T0193570

LIFE CYCLE TOOL
WorkBook and Guide

LIFE CYCLE TOOL
WorkBook and Guide

MELVORA "MICKIE" JACKSON

LIFE CYCLE TOOL WORKBOOK AND GUIDE

iUniverse books may be ordered through booksellers or by contacting:

iUniverse
1663 Liberty Drive
Bloomington, IN 47403
www.iuniverse.com
1-800-Authors (1-800-288-4677)

Because of the dynamic nature of the Internet, any web addresses or links contained in this book may have changed since publication and may no longer be valid. The views expressed in this work are solely those of the author and do not necessarily reflect the views of the publisher, and the publisher hereby disclaims any responsibility for them.

Any people depicted in stock imagery provided by Thinkstock are models, and such images are being used for illustrative purposes only. Certain stock imagery © Thinkstock.

ISBN: 978-1-5320-3319-3 (sc)
ISBN: 978-1-5320-3320-9 (e)

Print information available on the last page.

iUniverse rev. date: 10/12/2017

CONTENTS

Preface ix

Introduction xi

Acknowledgments xvii

Section 1
Creating Your Life Cycle Tool............................ 1

This workbook helps you decide what to do with your life. In this section, you learn how attitude, behavior, anger, consequences, and solutions affect the outcome of your success.

Discover the answers to the following questions:

What is a life cycle tool?

How do I use this workbook?

What is the importance of developing self-image, self-confidence, and self-worth?

What is self-image?

What is self-confidence?

What is self-worth?

What are the don'ts?

What are the dos?

Section 2
Workbook Discover Your Self-Worth 11

Self-Evaluation

    Evaluating Yourself

Making a Life Change

Questions: Self-Evaluation Test

Your Self-Help LCTWBG–Evaluation Response

What is it that I like about my life right now?

Is there something that needs to change in my life?

Section 3
Your Self-Help Life Cycle Tool
Evaluation Responses 17

Choosing a New Life Goal

How to Plan for a New Life Goal

Creating Your Circle of Support

Section 4
Choosing a New Life Goal 21

What is my goal?

What tasks must I complete to obtain my goal?

What are my resources?

How do I move forward with my goals?

What are my target dates for my goals?

What changes can I expect to see?

Section 5
How Do I Reward Myself for
Completing My Goals? 27

How do I reward myself for completing my goals?

What would I like to do now that I have completed one of my goals?

What should I do when I feel down?

About the Author 29

PREFACE

After overlooking numerous financial and career opportunities, I compiled my greatest life experiences and years of academic study to help me think about how to best write this workbook. I felt it was my duty to help those who have lost hope and to bring to the surface a way for you to assess weaknesses and strengths that have kept you from reaching your full life potential. It's important to think about how often we fail to realize that our worst enemies can be ourselves. Having a clear understanding of these concepts will help you better cope with the internal and external challenges that interfere with your personal growth, employment success, and ability to contribute to the family support system.

Your self-esteem can often be damaged by loss of your support system, family, lost income, job layoff, divorce, or lack of parental support. I'm speaking from personal experiences. I struggled to figure out which road to take to achieve my life goals. After so many job layoffs, broken marriages, low-income status, and raising children as a single parent, I can safely say it is not an easy task to accomplish. It's been an ongoing life process with great challenges through it all. That's one reason I felt compelled to develop this workbook and guide to help you get started on your way to achieving your life goals.

If you take your time with this workbook, you'll understand why we feel stagnant at times in our lives. You'll learn how we can slowly move forward with help from loved ones and close friends who are willing to support our efforts to accomplish our goals. It is important to remember, though, that most of the work will be initiated by you. No more procrastination.

Writing this workbook and guide was challenging, as I currently have my own life struggles. I work full-time and have a part-time job to supplement my income because of job cutbacks and to help pay for my academic studies.

This workbook is also about building your self-image, self-confidence, and self-worth. Self-worth is an important part of your human development and helps build strong character. You need to understand these important tools when dealing with people in any type of relationship, including those associated with your employment, support system, church, or school. An important thing to remember is to stay focused on the solution to your life problems no matter what they are. Don't give up, and you can achieve your lifelong goals. Use this workbook and tool to help you accomplish what you need to do to reach your goals.

INTRODUCTION

Your Life Cycle Tool: Workbook and Guide helps guide your decision making. Let me show you how to use this workbook to your advantage by using the step-by-step guide to making life decisions less stressfully. Learn how to stay focused on the solution and not the problem when faced with life challenges. Using this workbook helps you understand and identify an easier way to approach your life problems. I suggest you read through the workbook, do the exercises, and read the responses. Write in the workbook. This is your personal journal for keeping track of your progress. You will learn a new way of thinking on how to approach and obtain your life goals.

Let's review what each section discusses.

Section 1: This lesson will cover the importance of self-image, self-confidence, and self-worth. These are vital to understanding how to build your self-worth. It is a character-building enhancement tool. Once you learn this life process, you are not up for negotiating with anyone. The don'ts and dos may or may not apply to you; it all depends on your stage of life. You could just need the right support system. Perhaps you need to change your environment. Change jobs. Remove yourself from a toxic, unhealthy relationship. Look the list over; you may discover it applies to you in one way or another. I suggest you read and reread each section for a better understanding of the process.

Section 2: This lesson reviews the importance of self-evaluation. A short test challenges you to think about making a life change if you need to. I suggest you take the test twice—maybe even three times—to see whether you get the same responses. This is helpful in clarifying what your goals should look like or become. I suggest you not jump ahead of the steps. It will only demonstrate that you aren't ready for change in your life right now and devalue the process for you.

Section 3: This lesson helps you begin to think about choosing a new life goal and the process that will take you there. You'll start to think about the things or people you need to eliminate in your life. They are toxic and will not support your efforts to approach life differently. Selecting the right person or persons for your support group is imperative to your success. Always refer to your notes, which will help you understand and see your progress.

Section 4: This lesson assists you in discovering which goal you should select first by its priority in your life at the time of working in this workbook. You'll learn to use the resources you already have at your disposal and how to utilize those that are conducive to your goal-setting approach. You'll need to implement time management in your life every day to keep yourself on track. Learn to develop a timeline so you can review what you've already done and not duplicate your work. Write in this workbook as much as possible to measure your progress daily or weekly as you work toward your goals. You can expect to see a new attitude toward life, a newfound spirit of inspiration, and the ability to stay focused and on task with regard to your goals.

Section 5: This is the final stage of the workbook. If you accomplish one goal in two weeks of reading and writing in the workbook, that is a major goal accomplishment, and you are seriously motivated to achieve your goals. No need to worry if you don't accomplish one goal in that time frame. Take your time. It's your life and your workbook; the slower the better.

Consider rewarding yourself with a small pleasure. Whatever it is that will take you out of your element for a little while—something like treating yourself to a movie, a nice dinner, a concert, or even a special trip. Try to have a level head about your choice of self-reward. You must stay on track, no matter what. If you feel down on some days because something or someone has caused you to get off your goal setting, refocus and call your support system. The special people you selected for your support system are there to encourage you to get back on track with your goals. So let's get started.

My Story

I grew up in Wisconsin. Yes, home of the Green Bay Packers, one of my favorite football teams. I came from a family of seven children. It was a two-parent family until I was eight years old. Both my parents taught the importance of family, community, and the Word of God.

I attended public schools there and was involved in every activity from Brownie to Girls Scouts. Then on to high school, where I was involved in extracurricular activities such as cheerleading, drill team, and choir. I was a star track-and-field athlete. Track and field was exciting to me. It took me to another dimension in life. I met all kinds of people from within and outside of Wisconsin. I started getting invited to parties of kids who had graduated high school and were attending college a hundred miles from where I lived. I was impressed with them because they made it into adulthood and were out on their own.

In November 1975, I decided it was time for me to move out of my mother's house and make a huge leap to California. I met some wonderful people who adopted me into their family, and we became one big, happy family. This is when I discovered I had a great, solid support system of people who also believed in family, attending church, and following God's doctrine. I managed two jobs while attending college for accounting, supporting myself, my own apartment, and my own job. It wasn't until 1982 that I really became interested in higher education while working at one of the biggest oil companies in the world in San Francisco, California. I later left the oil company and embarked on the human services field.

I earned an undergraduate degree from New College of California in psychology, with a specialization in humanities. I graduated from the University of San Francisco with a master's in public administration, with an emphasis in health services. Currently, I'm in professional studies for my PhD in nonprofit management with emphasis in human services.

I have worked in the field of psychology for more than twenty years with nonprofit and for-profit organizations, along with a county-held position. I've primarily worked as a mental health counselor and a mental health clinician. I currently work with the department of corrections as a forensic mental health clinician. I was a member of the county's Reducing Health Disparity Committee for eight years. I served as a member of the Community Advisory Board (CAB) under the California Assembly Bill (AB) 109, also known as the Public Safety Realignment Act, a law designed to reduce prison overcrowding and decrease recidivism through the use of innovative approaches to corrections and community reentry. For my work on CAB, I received an honorable certificate for active participation.

From 2010 to 2012, I participated as a stakeholder/ provider on the California Reducing Disparities Population Report Project (CRDP), working with community advocate Dr. V. Diane Woods of the African American Health Institute of San Bernadine County. For my work with the California Institute of Mental Health, I received a California Legislature Assembly Resolution from the Honorable Mariko Yamada of the Fourth Assembly district. I was a core planning team member for California's African American Leadership Training Project, a one-year assignment. My work earned certificates of appreciation for ongoing support to the African American consumer and leadership project training from the California Institute of Mental Health.

ACKNOWLEDGMENTS

It is important for me to acknowledge individuals who have made significant impacts on my life. The late Dr. Wayne Dyer is one. I've purchased all his books and attended some of his workshops. One of his favorite quotes I adore is, "If you change the way you look at things, the things you look at change." Dr. Maya Angelou wrote, "If you don't like something, change it, if you can't change it, change your attitude." First lady Eleanor Roosevelt told us, "No one can make you feel inferior without your consent." I live with these specials words in my heart. They are implanted there forever. So much so that I mentor my children and grandchildren, echoing these same words in their lives.

Whenever I'm invited to host or cohost a speaking engagement, I always open with an introduction to one of these great and passionate speakers. Their voices and presence will forever have a great impression in my heart. I've learned that sharing knowledge is powerful, especially when you have an audience and have captivated their mind-sets. In addition, they are putting into practice what life experiences you have shared about your journey. Through this, one can help make theirs a more constructive, conducive life-changing event rather than making the same mistakes in life repeatedly.

"Doing the same thing over and over again and expecting a different result is insane." Over the years, that quote has been attributed to many people, most often Albert Einstein but Benjamin Franklin as well; it may even be an old Chinese proverb. Regardless of who said it, how profound is that quote? I find it to be one of the life-changing events for me.

My sincere hope as a writer is that you allow this workbook to penetrate your mind so that you're able to grasp its concepts. Please write in it. That will be the only way you can capitalize on the relevance and richness of this lifelong learning process.

You must be able to step outside your comfort zone to explore who you really are. Life is about taking chances. Let this workbook be one of your choices to help get you going. So what are you waiting for? Start you journey now.

CREATING YOUR LIFE CYCLE TOOL

First, let's define the words we demonstrate in *Your Life Cycle Tool: Workbook and Guide.*

Attitude

- the way a person views something or tends to behave toward it, often in an evaluative way
- a facial expression that allows you to understand what's on a person's mind
- a body position indicating mood or emotion; that is, the way a person carries himself or herself

Behavior

- the way one behaves
- the action or reaction of a person in response to internal and external stimuli
- the manner of conducting oneself
- the observable activity of a human

1

- the unexpected reactions of others

Anger

- a strong feeling of displeasure or hostility
- to make angry; to enrage or provoke
- to have deep resentment
- rage and fury, implying intense, explosive, often destructive emotion
- to provoke to striking or physically harming others

Consequences

- results of attitude reflection, anger outcomes, behaviors exhibited as result of poor decision making and the type of solution you choose that impacts you throughout your life
- Questions
  - o What type of attitude do you have about life?
  - o What kind of anger do you display toward others?
  - o What is your basic attitude daily?
  - o What consequences has your attitude caused?

Solutions

- the methods or processes of solving problems
- the answers to or dispositions of problems
- the states of being dissolved
- the satisfaction of solving problems

Creating Your Life Cycle Workbook: Decide Who and What You Want to Be

This is your individualized life cycle tool.

Who should use this workbook?

- any age
- any gender
- single, married, divorced, have a significant other

This life cycle tool was created just for you! If life interruptions kept you from reaching your goals, this workbook is for you.

This life cycle tool can help you start believing in yourself and understand you are in control of how your life can be. It can help you see yourself as a determined, capable person. You can embrace life fully with self-respect and love. You will see your goals are obtainable; even amid failures and mistakes, you can do it.

Why do we believe this is possible? As a self-starter, I have survived many life challenges and narrow roads. That is why today I can share my experiences, knowledge, and successes.

It's important to understand that creating goals for your life means you have a purpose. *Your Life Cycle Tool: Workbook and Guide* was created to help you get started on your way.

Jessica A. Jonikas, MA, Judith A. Cook, PhD, and Melvora Jackson, MPA, Phdc, Andriukaitis, Beall, Nobiling, Vogel–Scibilia (2004, 2015).

What Is a Life Cycle Tool?

A tool to help you set your life goals.

A life cycle tool guides you to understand what your life goals are and how to obtain them.

This is a plan for what you want to do with your life, regardless of age or gender. It helps you look at areas where you want to set new goals or make changes in your life.

Some of these areas are as follows:

1. Where you live
2. Who you spend your time with
3. Where you get services and support
4. Where you work or go to school/college
5. Change of employment/career
6. Improving or creating a healthy relationship

It may seem a little overwhelming to think about all these things at first. But it helps to remember that nobody makes his or her life changes all at once. It's easier to select the most obtainable goal first and then move on to the next one that is more challenging and time consuming. This is how you gain more success with *Your Life Cycle Tool: Workbook and Guide.*

It is important to remember that the average person completes at least one goal every day without knowing it. Think about this for a moment. You probably do a lot of things every day, like shower, eat breakfast, read a paper, go to work/school, or watch your favorite program on television. We don't usually think about these things as goals, but they are. So you already have some history of setting and reaching for your goals.

Most people's life goals are built on small goals leading to a larger goal.

What does this mean for me?

- I must do some things I don't want to do in order to obtain my goals.
- I must take some responsibility for my goal setting.
- I must understand it may feel scary or risky to try something new.
- I must develop trusting relationships to help support my goals.
- I can change my mind, slow things down, or speed things up when needed.
- I can take a short break from my plan if I feel overwhelmed.
- I set the pace because this is my life cycle tool plan.

How do I use this life cycle tool?

- Read the workbook before you write down your goals and tasks.
- Choose at least one person to support you in this process.

- Set aside time each day to go through your workbook to make plans and to review how you're progressing.
- Work on only one or two pages at a time, especially when you first start.
- Talk to a mentor or close friend about your goals.

Please note many people find it easier to talk with someone they trust.

What else do I need to know?

We've all be there. We make a promise to ourselves that this year will be different. We'll lose weight, we'll exercise, we'll make a friend, take a trip, start school. You name it, we said it before. Right?

What you need to know is there are many reasons we give up on our goals. But the main one is that we're simply not ready for change. Other reasons include

- trying to do too much too fast,
- getting discouraged by others, and
- not taking care of ourselves on the way.

If we fail, we feel worse, and the cycle continues with no progress at all.

Slow is always better.

The Mind is everything.

Humans are spiritual beings and the mind is our essence. We are undergoing spiritual trainings to polish our mind and return to the Spirit World with higher state of mind and learn awareness that benefits our lives and the ones we love.

Everything is subject to the cause and effect, so when we change our thoughts and our state of mind, our human relationships, health and financial circumstances change too. The cause of pain and suffering do not lie with others or the outside world but are created by ourselves. Therefore, we need to reflect on our thoughts and consciousness and correct them through our own effort.

Life is a workbook of problems to be solved.

Everyone experiences troubles and hardships as a part of living in this world.

We would all like to dismiss them if possible, however, the process of solving our problems in life will not go away. This requires various experiences and learn many different lessons. These experiences and lessons are nourishments for the soul's growth. Suffering hardships and difficulties are opportunities for growth. Once we are aware that "Life is a workbook" there is no longer any need to lament. Meaning-why do I have to be put through this suffering, when confronted with difficulties and hardships. Instead these are opportunities to learning that we come to ask ourselves what it is that we can learn from them.

Suffering is an opportunity to reflect on the mistakes of our own mind and thus free ourselves from self-punishment.

Experiences come from overcoming suffering because it creates "wisdom"

Through suffering and hardship, we can find seeds of happiness and spiritual healing and growth.

Happy Science North America (2014)

Self-Image

Self-image is the idea a person has of his or her own abilities, appearance, and personality. It is developed through self-assurance.

Self-Confidence

Self-confidence is the feeling of trust in one's abilities; qualities, judgments, morals, self-assurance, assertiveness, and self-reliance. It is developed by trusting yourself and your own judgment.

Self-Worth

Self-worth is the sense of one's personal value or worth as a person. It is developed by understanding how you build your self-image, having developed your self-confidence and evolving to your self-worth.

Don'ts

Don't allow anyone to make you feel inadequate because of their shortcomings.

Don't take on other people's perceptions of you.

Don't listen to the negative voices in your head.

Don't feel you are alone, ever.

Don't allow anyone to get you off track in achieving your goals.

Dos

Do think of yourself as a person with a life plan.

Do build on what you have, and enhance what you don't have.

Do keep moving forward, and surround yourself with like-minded people.

Do understand your self-worth.

Do believe in yourself.

WORKBOOK DISCOVER YOUR SELF-WORTH

Try to be a rainbow in someone's cloud.

—Maya Angelou

Evaluating Yourself

A self-test creates awareness of your thought processes in dealing with attitude, behavior, and anger. It can help pinpoint approaches to consequences and solutions.

Making a Life Change

Take small steps at first. Everyone has setbacks along the way, no matter how hard they may try or how good the plans are. Learning to reset life goals can help.

Staying on task with your life goals is imperative to your success.

Whatever changes you hope to make, you'll go through a process to achieve your goal. James Prochaska and his colleagues call this the "Stage of Change Model." This model has been utilized to help understand how life change works in many areas, including smoking, dieting, and substance abuse.

Reference: James O. Prochaska, PhD, & Carlo C. DiClemente, PhD., the stages of change model.

http://www.prochange.com/transtheoretical-model-of-behavior-change.

If you aren't ready for change and people around you are prospering, you should consider reevaluating your priorities.

Self-Evaluation Test

Circle yes, no, or don't know.

1. Do you feel a change would make your life better, happier, or easier?

Yes   No   Don't Know

2. Have you been thinking lately about one specific thing in your life you don't like or would like to change?

Yes   No   Don't Know

3. Do you intend to start planning within the next ninety days exactly what you must do to start making a change?

Yes   No   Don't Know

4. Have you already started to make changes in your life to make it easier, happier, or better?

Yes   No   Don't Know

Questions

1. How should I prioritize my thinking regarding my goals?

2. How do I get ready to make and use *Your Life Cycle Tool: Workbook and* Guide?

3. How do I create my circle of support?

4. How do I consider change and choose a life goal?

5. How should I plan for a new goal or life change?

6. How do I act on a new goal or life change?

7. How do I maintain my goal to achieve success?

8. How do I move forward?

Where am I in the change process?

1. Where should I begin to look at the change that is needed right now?

2. How do I make a new friend?

3. How can I get better control of my health?

4. How can I lose or gain weight?

5. How can I get a job or create self-employment (entrepreneurial) opportunities?

6. Should I go to school to earn a certificate or college degree?

YOUR SELF-HELP LIFE CYCLE TOOL EVALUATION RESPONSES

If you answered yes to one of the first two questions (or both), you probably are in the considering a life change stage (stage 2) process. In this stage, you are focused on gathering information about the change you want to make and on weighing the pros and cons of change. As you consider what change will mean for you, some helpful strategies would be to

a) hear other people talk about their success stories,

b) receive encouragement from people who've been there already and learn what it took for them to make changes, and

c) receive information about approaches or other options.

Many people stay in the second stage for a long time before they are ready to move into actual planning and action for change. If this happens to you, don't worry; it's common. The more you consider your options, the easier it will be once you are ready to plan and act on your goals.

As mentioned previously, all changes require going through a process. The basic idea behind James Prochaska and colleagues' Stages of Change Model is that when we are faced with changing our lives in some way, we need first to figure out what stage of change we are in. This helps us decide whether we're ready to make change, and what we need to do to succeed if we are ready.

If you answered yes to the first three questions (or just the third one), you are probably in the preparing for a life change stage (stage 3). In this stage, you mostly need to define tasks and find tools and resources to support your specific life change. Family members, peers, providers, and other supporters need to know you're ready for a change. They can help you remember that you may need to try many things before finding the best options for your situation. In this stage, you'll also need to reward yourself for small steps you make.

If you answered yes to all four questions (or just the fourth one), you're probably in the acting on a life change stage (stage 4). In this stage, you need support and encouragement for changes you've already made. The plans you have for maintaining success over time will enhance your ability to build self-confidence, which will help you develop self-worth.

In all the stages of change, attending your self-help support group is crucial for your well-being. This is especially recommended in the fourth stage.

If you answered no or don't know to any of the questions, you may not be ready to consider or prepare for a life change now. That's okay. It's better to know where you are than have change forced upon you. This can be discouraging. But don't worry. Finish reading this workbook because you may find that as you gain more information and skills, you'll become ready to consider planning and able to act on your goals to make a change.

What do I like about my life right now?

I have a great support system.
I like my job.
I like where I work.
I like where I live.
I am in a healthy relationship.
I feel good about myself.

Is there something in my life that needs to change right now?

I need a better job.
I'd like a nicer place to live.
I need a change in school.
I'd like a new relationship.
I need a good support system.

What one important change do I need to make now?

What are your thoughts?

CHOOSING A NEW LIFE GOAL

This is where you start to really think about what you would like to do with your life and what goals are obtainable at this point in your life. Let's think about a few simple goals.

Goal 1: What is it that you see in your life right now that needs to be changed? Anything stand out for you? If so, what?

- Decide what is most important to work on first.
- Look at the things going well in your life.
- Build on your strengths, and then focus on areas that need improvement.
- Are you really ready to create a change in your life?

How should I plan for a new life goal?

What are the desired results of this action plan?

What should I do first?

What tools do I need to succeed?

What is my financial budget to complete the task?

What kind of life interruption can I expect to happen?

What does my support system look like?

When should I seek help if I feel stuck?

Creating Your Circle of Support

Who should be in my circle of support?

- someone who is very supportive of my goals
- someone who encourages me to strive every day to achieve goals
- someone I can trust
- someone who will understand my struggles, challenges, and desired ambitions
- someone who has experienced life hardships and struggles but, regardless of these things, succeeded with his or her life goals

Make sure you have every means of communication to contact your support person or group.

Steps to Planning Your Life Goal Outline

My goal is to do what?

_____

_____

_____

_____

_____

_____

_____

_____

What are the tasks necessary to obtaining my goal?

- Find employment.
- Create or update résumé.
- Create a cover letter.
- Seek advice from temporary employment agencies.
- Apply at workforce development office near my home or city or another county.
- Seek online help from sites such as CareerBuilder, Monster Jobs, and Craigslist.

- Meet with career counselor at employment agency or school.
- Undergo counseling to learn new skills on how to develop healthy relationships.
- Attend workshops on nutritional and lifestyle habits.
- Attend cognitive management therapy.

What are my resources?

_____

_____

_____

_____

_____

_____

Moving Forward with My Goals

What are my target dates for completing my goals?

_____

_____

_____

_____

_____

_____

What changes can I expect to see?

_____

_____

_____

_____

_____

_____

_____

_____

_____

_____

HOW DO I REWARD MYSELF FOR COMPLETING MY GOALS?

What things would I like to do now that I have completed one of my goals?

_____

_____

_____

_____

_____

_____

_____

_____

_____

_____

_____

_____

What should I do when I feel down?

I can contact someone from my support group to discuss my feelings.

Remember: this workbook was created to help you understand that life offers us hardships and struggles. How we handle them and their outcomes reflect how we think.

Additional Writing Space

_____

_____

_____

_____

_____

_____

_____

_____

_____

_____

_____

ABOUT THE AUTHOR

Melvora "Mickie" Jackson has an MPA degree in management and human services and a BA in psychology and humanities. She is pursuing a doctorate in nonprofit management.

Jackson has worked professionally in the field of psychology for more than twenty-eight years in nonprofit and for-profit organizations, along with county positions. She, her daughter, and their dog, Frankie, live in Northern California.

Printed in the United States
By Bookmasters